Rhythms in Caribbean Poetry

Ras Bongle I

Editing / Book Layout by

Passionate Words Editing Services

(IG @passionate.words.editing246)

DEDICATION

Special dedication to my brethren Sean Leach and big sis Donna –
you will always be remembered. Rest in peace.

CONTENTS

Introduction — 11

Editorial Review — 13

Ancestral Rhythms — 15

As Far As The Eyes Can See — 16

Our Motherland Africa — 19

Pun Dat Ship — 21

No Place Called Home — 22

Dat Old Cane Mill — 24

I Weep For Them — 25

How Could I Forget (I) — 26

Our Story — 28

Illusions In The Dark — 31

Land Ship Sailing, Ahoy — 33

Landship Sailing Again — 35

How Do I Forget? — 36

Positive Rhythms — 38

Tribute To The Highest One — 39

Echoes of Blackness — 40

Darkened Vibrations — 41

Mother Of Mothers — 42

Tribute To Grans — 44

How Can I Forget   45

Giving Thanks to the Gods   46

Awareness   48

Beliefs   49

God's Greatness   50

Expressions of Righteousness   52

Natural Rhythms   **53**

Deep Down In De Dirt   54

Expressions of Beauty   56

Nature   57

Mother Nature   58

Sounds of Nature   60

Our Springs   61

Doves Cooing   63

Reef Warriors   64

Natural Living   66

Litter Bug   67

Nature's Rains   69

Mother Nature I   71

Modern-Day Rhythms   **72**

The Struggle   73

How Many More Tears   75

Money Lovers   77

How Far Did We Come from?   79

SELF MADE PRISON   81

Oh How I Wish   83

Pain   85

Reality   86

Clinic Wait   88

Clinic   90

Dat Ting Call Wuk   91

Over Time   93

Unjust People   95

Abuse   97

Have You Ever Wondered?   99

Dis Money Ting   102

Money, Money, Money   104

A Long Short Story   106

Running down Money   108

Looking Within   110

Classes   112

Guns   115

What We Were Taught   117

Gran Son   120

Poor People's Voices 123

Money Effect 125

Keys 127

Curious George 129

Money Control 131

Think It Through 133

Why the Rush? 135

Last Day of 2018 137

Frustration 138

Cry of the Poor 140

Christmas 2018 142

Reaching Out 144

Learning More 146

Untrue Leaders 150

Island Rhythms 152

These Shores 153

Zr Squeeze 156

Oistins Fish Festival2018 159

At the Garrison 162

Barbados 164

Where Barbados Gone? 166

Politics 2018 169

Tourist White Man   171

Chibim   173

Granny and Ms. Prime Minister   175

Our Prime Minister   177

Q in the Community   179

We Gatherin' 2020   181

Glossary   **183**

INTRODUCTION

This book is written primarily in Bajan dialect. The rhythms and cadence of the author's flowing speech are the highlight of this work.

The English version of the words that are printed in Bajan dialect will be highlighted for those who do not understand Bajan language directly.

Not everyone can recognise Nature's call when they hear or see it at its very best, yet Nature's call is around us every day – even at night – as we see and hear the activities of different species of animals and plants displaying themselves in the most harmonious ways.

Nature's call sounds both like songs that we are familiar with and some new and unknown.

Each time we take a deep breath of Nature, it somehow soothes away the hardship and troubles that are displayed by people in the world and around us. When we really take the time out and listen to observe and grasp Nature as it fills up the atmosphere with sweet, genuine calls, we feel peace.

We in the Caribbean are indeed blessed by Nature. Many people in the world have never seen or experienced Nature like this, which is expressing itself in many different ways. This book tells us of this land and the Caribbean as she presents herself.

All she is asking us to do is to preserve and not destroy.

Everything written in this book pertains to Barbadian and Caribbean culture. Some of the events described took place long ago and some are more recent; all are true stories written in poetic form. The book tells of the every day life styles of Bajan and Caribbean people.

In these stories, we have heard of the cruelty of our ancestors back then. Also, the hidden truths (that many don't know about and we have tried to carefully research) tell us where we came from, who we were and who we have become as a direct result of such a past. Additionally, these stories tell us who we still are and where we are going. We recognise as a result of extensive research that the stories about ourselves that we have been taught only tell us half of our story; when we only settle for half of our story, we accomplish little knowledge of ourselves. And, at the same time, we will still give in to the inheritors of our colonial masters, who still rule in some form or the other.

EDITORIAL REVIEW

'Rhythms in Caribbean Poetry' is deceptively simple. Most of the poems' lines are rhyming couplets and the language is simple and straightforward. But this is the essence of the book, and the author.

A man of the land and sea, as evidenced by poems such as "Deep Down in De Dirt" and "Reef Warriors", the author delves into some pretty heavy topics, such as slavery ("Pun Dat Ship", "Dat Old Cane Mill" and African pride ("Echoes of Blackness"), family ("Tribute to Grans"), the harshness of every day life and even the politics of the day ("Politics 2018", "Granny and Ms. Prime Minister", "Our Prime Minister") in his native Barbados.

The cadence of Barbadian speech (commonly referred to by the more colloquial 'Bajan') rings through this entire collection. The author immediately tells the reader that the book is in Bajan dialect, for the most part, and helpfully provides a glossary of Bajan words at the end of the text. The title is apt, as one familiar with a Bajan accent can hear it through the words written.

'Rhythms in Caribbean Poetry' is a slice of history from the eyes of a man who loves his African heritage ("Our Motherland Africa", loves his family, loves nature and loves his country ("Barbados", "Where Barbados Gone?", even when he is bemoaning the harsh realities of working hard but seeing very little return ("Dat Ting Called Wuk", "Overtime", "Poor People Voices").

As I arranged the poems into the specific sections and created the layout, I was struck with the sense of the African inspired idea of looking back to go forward, or *sankofa*. Indeed, in researching 'sankofa' I learned that it was a Tiwi word loosely meaning 'to retrieve'. It was interesting to learn that the word is literally translated from an Akan proverb *"Se wo were fi na wosan kofa a yenkyiri,"* meaning, "It is not taboo to go back for what you forgot (or left behind)."[1]

This book is a love letter to the rhythms of life seen through the eyes of one who tells it like it is, and who is giving us a slice of history with which we can chart our way forward.

 I enjoyed working on this book and look forward myself to seeing it go far in showcasing Bajan life upon an international stage.

Robert R. Gibson

Editor
Passionate Words Editing Services

---

[1] Taken from 'About Sankofa - What does Sankofa Mean; Stockton Univeristy (https://www.stockton.edu/sankofa/about.html#:~:text=Sankofa%20(SAHN%2Dkoh%2Dfah, Sankofa%20is%20a%20phrase%20that)

ANCESTRAL RHYTHMS

As Far As The Eyes Can See

As far as the eyes can see -

Let's take a look into our story.

Beginning long ago, with you and me,

Where they came and tek 'way even granny;

Then give it a name and call it slavery.

Taken from the east and brought to the west,

Bound and tied with a heavy load on me chest.

Bundled together and feeling the pain;

And those who fell asleep were quickly slain.

Belly starving and can't eat anything for long,

Only to stare at one another while they sing their song.

As far as the eyes can see -

Listen carefully to our story.

It's a story of a land that we still know,

Where the pillars of the earth meet and waters sweetly flow.

Flowing with streams of naturalness,

Sustaining life and making us blessed.

Some of us will never see her again,

Many of us will never feel her rain;

For many were lost and scattered about,

Even lost in our minds; we caan' even shout!

For four hundred years wishing the pain would go away -

Yet buried in I and so it will stay.

As far as the eyes can see -

They brought us into this country.

So many came and born after them,

Not knowing the truth and how we could mend,

With minds so tainted to fight against one another –

That's how he enslaved us to even kill our brother!

As far as the eyes can see –

One shout, "Ahoy! Land must be …"

With licks on our backs we came off that ship,

Hand and foot bound, still feeling the whip.

Then to a place where we were all sold,

Staring at each other as our lives did unfold.

As far as the eyes can see –

 Look what really happen to we!

Now today they say we are free,

Yet we feel like we are still in slavery

All over again, this time only to get by,

And salary so small, only to fly…

But that ain't all of the story, massa at the end got paid,

To rob and enslave us with all the money they made.

Now they're all set up big here in this very land,

Holding down the businesses by their ancestors' firm hand.

Expecting us the offspring of their oppressors to still go and work for them,

Yet I say to each and every black person, "Always remember WHEN!"

Our Motherland Africa

O, I dream of a land far, far away – that land where great stories are told,

A land that dwells from the beginning of time; a place ancient and old.

That land I have not seen with my eyes, I can say –

I have only seen her in my heart, that land so far away.

What does it mean to feel her warmth? Just to see her with my eyes?

A joy it would be after so long, even to see her deep blue skies.

Yes, she means everything to me, from where my ancestors came,

Those who are kings and queens of the world, for the cosmic has born each name.

So how can I forget the place where I came from?

The place that still plays the great conga drum –

And everything that I have ever known of her

Was taken all away and replaced for a 'sir';

They try their very best to erase her from my heart,

But deep down inside we could never depart,

For she runs through my bloodline for ever and ever,

And I will never let her go – no, not never!

We have come so far and told so many lies;

Our great, great granny, we can still hear her cries –

Ras Bongle I

Those cries that burn deep within each and every heart,

Yes, those cries you could hear from the time slavery start!

 The cry that says, "Let's fight the fight!"

Not with fists only, but with insight.

The fight for equal rights for all,

That fight for all humanity to stand tall,

So that the land that I dream of so far, far away,

I still call her my home; forever, that's how I will stay!

Pun Dat Ship

Pun dat ship, dat stinking ship,

Hand and foot bound today; ah still feeling every dip.

Brother pun me right, sista pun me left,

And this big monster – oh, it feels like death!

With de stench of some of those who have passed

Then thrown overboard or beaten on the mast.

Oh, how we look on with dismay at their brutalness,

Can't do a thing but hold de load pun me chest.

Their brutality never seems to ever go away,

And at the mercy of the pirates, that was our stay.

Bound and helpless with nothing on our backs,

Nothing to eat as we lay flat.

Sad is that story pun dat stinking ship,

All memories of sadness with dat stinking whip.

It's always good to know where you came from;

Where time has began and we can call her 'mom'.

So look into yourself and stop adopting his style,

Ours is here forever – his is only for a while.

So how can I forget dat stinking ship?

Hand and foot still tied and today feeling every dip!

No Place Called Home

They took me from my birth into captivity,

And brought me to a place where I did not want to be –

Then call it my home.

When I got there, with nothing on me back,

With a huge heavy load, and dem bastards won't slack;

Beating me from start until end –

Some mental scars in life surely have no friend –

Still they call this my home.

My whole family I left back there,

Never to see them again is my greatest fear.

We all loved our village, we lived so free,

Now destruction from the beast makes us all flee!

Fleeing for our lives from his great big gun,

So many dead – got us on the run –

Yet they call this my home.

By trickery and greed this monster came,

Looking to conquer and looking for fame.

To enslave my people, to treat I like this,

Taking away my pride, joy and happiness –

Still they call this my home.

If the tables were turned I am sure they wouldn't like:

They came to change the world by falsehoods and fights.

I am here to preserve and not to destroy,

For even in this place I still find my own joy.

So you can take I to any part of the earth,

Wherever I go blackness will always rebirth.

For I am the earth and the earth am I —

Always look to our elders, for we'll never die!

Dat Old Cane Mill

Oh how I nearly brek me back pun dat old cane mill from morn til evening come,

Wukking sa hard bringing dem canes up de hill before de sun ga dun.

This is de norm every day fa me ya see,

Wukking on massa plantation in his slavery.

We bend our backs hard in de boiling sun,

Doing all his wuk til de evening come.

Everywhere we look there is more wuk my friend,

We have ta grind dem canes until it all end.

every day we have fa wuk real hard pun dat old cane mill,

With bellies starving; this ain't no thrill.

When de evening dun and things coming to an end,

Anything ta eat is truly a godsend.

Just ta ease ma belly lil bit from de pain,

For tomorrow wuk starts all over again.

I Weep For Them

I weep for them, my brethren, my friends,

Who have travelled so far, how could we mend?

How could we mend those scars from yesteryear?

Scars from the past, today, they still so clear!

These scars will never fade away,

They will live with us until we go some day.

Deep scars that will reach the end of time.

To seek the truth, how can we find?

Scars of a place that we were bought and bred,

Sold to the highest bidder and hardly being fed.

Scars of horror that would make your head spin,

Who try to escape shot dead and say he sin!

This rock is too small to escape from them,

With so much plantations, we have to find a friend.

Fear makes man shut up his mouth,

Not even in his hut he can't even shout.

"Don't utter a word," mamma would always say,

"If anyone know, massa will be on his way.

To take any one of us with no questions asked,

And seeing you again will be a thing of the past!"

So I weep for them, my brother, my friend,

We've all come this far, but together, we'll blend.

How Could I Forget (I)

How could I forget de days when de whip and de gun did rule,

And we would get treat even worse than a mule?

How could I forget -

When we wuk so hard til we hands did bleed,

Hoeing, forking and planting massa seed.

Looka dem days, na! Wa, ah can't forget dem days!

How could I forget -

When we wuk all day till de evening gone down

Not a drop a wata - some fall ta de ground

Dem was some days, nah? Dem was some days!

How could I forget when John brek a piece of de massa cane?

Massa chop off he hand and leave he in pain.

How sad dat was, nah? Oh, how sad!

How could I forget -

How we as little ones had ta go and wuk in de field,

Wuk all day and could never see a meal.

How could I forget -

When de horse and de dogs get treat betta than we

While we sit in their dark thing call slavery

How could I forget? Why must I forget?

Our Story

Why fight down my brother who is from another land?

Skin dark like mine from the sun, sea and sand.

We are all from one place, only different tribes are we.

All of us are one big family; come, I'll help you to see.

In ancient times we all would unite,

For there was no war, not a battle in sight.

All just live in peace and truth,

Trodding Jah's way early, from youths.

Those days still live deep down in my heart,

And never will I let them depart.

It is true tribal wars began long after that time,

Through ignorance of thinking peace was not on the decline.

Those days were just before the white man came,

While tribes had many captives, he just played his money game.

Every time he came, he was making more plans,

To enslave all my people and to take away their lands.

Running after his world of fame,

Bringing only destruction in his terror of rain.

Our sweet Mother Africa never the same,

As we were bundled on those ships with our faces in shame.

A price of life from one man to another -

That man he just killed? He was my brother!

Then to take us to another part of the world,

On a ship's voyage that will make us curl…

Curl into a ball of pain and distress

And in a place where we still have no rest.

I am one of the many of whom have survived,

For who fell sick on the journey, sharks ate alive.

Now hardship and suffering are what I have been through;

Since they brought us here we were all told what to do

For we no longer make our own rules,

Massa makes them and calls us, his slaves, fools.

Just praying one day for a change in time

Where those who come after us full freedom they will find

And as we live our lives, the journey will be eased,

And for the end of slavery, we will no longer fall at his needs.

For this story must be told to all the young,

For our ancestors who had to be strong.

For never again must we ever let this thing proceed

Robbing us of land and life just to satisfy their greed.

Can't hide the truth forever, for our story must be told,

So our young ones will know how our ancestors were sold.

Taken away by force they went,

Ras Bongle I

With the driving of the whips on their backs were bent.

So little ones let them tell you – no lie –

Many have fought and many have died.

Their quest was never to let us go free –

Yet with the gods on our side so we will be!

Illusions In The Dark

Deep in my sleep, deep in the dark,

There are voices heard, each playing their part.

Shouts and screams, anguish, and cries,

Answers untold as they all wonder why.

Never to be seen again in this life,

Yet their voices are heard as they go down with strife.

Some say I hear voices here and there,

Still their voices are heard so loud, so clear.

Crystal clear, they speak deep from the dark,

Of the shadowy grave, in the belly of the shark.

After being half dead in the dungeon of the beast,

Some were thrown overboard to be the shark's new feast.

Oh the journey was a rough and difficult trod,

Hands and feet tied, still beaten by the rod.

That one continued and never stopped;

The whip was constant, until some people dropped.

The stench of faeces was everywhere,

No food to eat, they could only stare,

At my brothers and sisters with heads hold down –

Still wondering what happened, what really went wrong?

Well, it's all in the greed of the money they seek –

Sharks they are; their maker they shall meet.

Not only those who made it can tell the tale:

For the dead of my people do speak - their voices have not failed!

Land Ship Sailing, Ahoy

Look at we Landship[2] coming just sailing – ahoy!

With old and young together dancing with joy!

Movements on display for everyone to see,

Every time I see them it makes me feel happy.

It is true, this is our Bajan thing – original from the start –

Which each and every Bajan should hold dearly to their heart!

Our people brought this from Africa with broken hearts as time went by,

Expressing themselves with things that are true. Praise to God in the highest high!

Why let go of our Landship? Is this not where heritage grew?

Plaiting that maypole with ribbons helps make our spirits renew!

Each act tells a story in its own unique way,

Through them our ancestors do speak, and they have much to say.

Listen carefully to the tuk – what a joy to hear,

Dem dress up so sweet, all eyes have to stare!

Our Landship must live on, family, even when we leave

[2] Landship – Barbadian cultural organisation formed in the 1860's by retired seamen who attempted to retain the camaraderie they had while at sea. It is most known for its public performances. (Barbados Museum & Historical Society - https://www.facebook.com/barbadosmuseum/posts/the-landship-is-an-organization-founded-in-the-1860s-by-retired-seamen-as-an-att/10152044812953383/)

this rock -

So it's time to show the world we Landship is what Bajans got!

Let's thank our ancestors every time we see our Landship sailing in,

And let's give our support for the sweet joy that it does surely bring!

Who are not with us, well that is their thing –

For in my eyes, with all respect, Landship will always win.

So, people, let us continue to love and support them all the way,

For in my heart our sweet Landship for sure will always stay.

Landship Sailing Again

Again, look we Landship come sailing – ahoy!

To each and every Bajan spreading so much joy.

Everywhere them land I have to be there,

Pure sweetness and love envelop the atmosphere.

A special group of people who ain't forget where they came from –

The place that started with the real conga drum.

Portraying the wear of the colonial masters, some of us will say,

Yet each dance spells out our freedom in a unique, special way.

Each manoeuvre is showing the world one day we will overcome,

The pain and suffering as some still toil in the burning sun.

Every move should remind us of what we have been through,

Neatly the poles are plaited to make our spirits renew.

Little ones hold on to our Landship with truly all of your hearts,

For our ancestral spirit of righteousness in us will surely never depart.

Through this thanking them for guiding us all along

So we'll always be holding on to our Landship with our ancestral African song.

How Do I Forget?

Oh what a life that we have all lived from the days of young until old,

With all the stories that we have heard yet the truth has never been told.

At times we do forget where we came from and, as a result, why we are here,

A people of great resilience and, with God, we carry no fear.

Some of us as we live our lives can only see good at the end,

And through it all as we seek the truth, sometimes, we only need a friend.

A friend in need is a friend indeed -

But there will not be such until we sow that seed:

That seed of righteousness that will endure,

Which will keep our lives flowing for ever more.

Endurance from our existing mental whips and chains,

We have come this far - it is brewed in our veins.

That blood that holds us yet so close,

In one accord, still no man boasts.

To forget will never ever hide her face,

Yet I carry no anger within my space.

I choose to forgive just to free my mind,

And forever seek God's love my true divine.

Yet with patience I will continue to answer my ancestors cry,

Coming from them is the truth, in which I know I can rely.

POSITIVE RHYTHMS

Tribute To The Highest One

Of all the things that I can do

I'll praise Thee, Lord, yes, I'll praise you.

In all the thoughts that I could know,

Only causes me to praise Thee more.

Even in times of hardship and in pain,

It's only with Thine love that I can gain.

Thou enchanted one, who is always true,

Who has set us free – oh, I love you!

For no other one will I make such a claim,

For in my heart, Thou art always the same.

So as I focus on Thee in this time,

Show me Thy ways, oh sweet Divine!

Reveal Thine knowledge of wisdom of old,

Gird I with strength such as to behold

The strength to do what is just and right,

That my life will be pure and true in thy sight.

This will always be my prayer, my Lord,

To serve you always for thou are my God.

Raise true righteousness deep down from the ground,

Filling hearts and minds, let it all abound.

Spreading enchanted days of Africanness again,

And of your love and faithfulness, we can never refrain.

Echoes of Blackness

Glittering echoes of blackness that never stop being heard,

Shining so bright in darkness, silent without a word.

Sparkling in the sun that will every morning rise,

Oh beautiful blackness, you are no surprise.

Taken from the east and brought to the west

By men on their great, evil quest.

Men who love to brag and boast

'Bout the journeys they make and who made the most.

With cruelty on our backs, so we stand,

For blackness will never die, such is the master's plan.

Our gods who started all blackness in time,

With blackness you do find light, yes, both of them we can find.

This great light of blackness stretches far and wide,

This great light of blackness surely cannot hide.

This precious light of blackness cannot be erased,

This precious light of blackness will always hold its space.

Glittering light of blackness we hear your cry,

From the cuts of the whip to the raping of our children, we still ask why.

Glittering echoes of blackness, your time is now,

To regain the crown that you have lost – we honour you as we take that bow.

Darkened Vibrations

Times of joy, times of sad,

Darkened vibrations make me feel so glad.

Where vibrations of darkness are deep in my soul,

Back in the Motherland where everything was gold.

We all chant and sing to the rhythm of the drum,

As we all live together, unity always around.

Rhythm of darkness, chanting green,

Blue light magic on the mountain seen.

From far across where the yellow moon shines

So crystal clear, where peace is divine.

Darkened vibrations, how everything glows,

Even in the darkest dark where the riverbed flows.

We see darkness of red deep within the shade,

It looks like a rainbow, it's wonderfully made.

Sweet, darkened vibrations, where pure love abounds,

Once unity was sure, everyone was sound.

But we fell for tricks as we welcomed him,

Then by force took us to this place we now call Bim.

Darkened vibrations come from deep and far,

Pureness of light, that is who we are.

Darkened vibrations in the morning light,

Shining so sweet shining so bright.

Light through darkness that will never fade,

Light of life in darkness, yes, we are wonderfully made.

Mother Of Mothers

Oh, mother of mothers, who has borne us all, bless us from the African sun.

Sweet mother of ours, love from you is where all life began.

There is no one else that can bear the pain, who has born us all,

With all the truth that one can find, you have answered every call.

Great mother who always dries our tears, each trial along life's way,

You are always willing to help us all as we journey night and day.

So many stories are told of your acts of grace, which are always tried and true,

Of all the gifts that life could give, mom, we are glad that we were given you.

Mother of creation, mother of the world, all of ours we give with grace,

Mother of salvation, mother of the earth, the sun has seen your face!

Who has forgotten you has truly forgotten themself.

Eyes darkened by their shadows while running after their wealth,

Mother of mothers, we all know for you there is no end -

You are forever our sweet mother and will always be our loving friend.

Tribute To Grans

Oh granny, how you treat me so sweet,

Take care of me from young, give me food to eat!

My sweet granny, you never put me wrong,

By de sweat of your brow, you have made me strong.

Granny, how could I forget those days with you?

'Specially on Sundays when I taste your sweet stew?

How many hearts out there like my loving gran?

She stood up to the test, she stood up to the plan.

When no one else gave much confidence,

Granny just so cool, taking no offence.

She had loved us all from the very start,

And my love for her will never depart.

Even when her flesh at sometime in life would decay,

My love for her will forever stay.

For when the road get rough and things get mean,

Then granny spiritually shows up on life's journey's scene.

Guiding us when times are just not so nice,

Telling us to hold on, make the sacrifice.

Gran, had not for your wisdom, today where would I be?

You have opened my eyes, cause me to see

The truth and what you have been through.

The good that you stand for, we will always honour you.

How Can I Forget

How can I forget the struggles that we have been through,

Back in the days when granny help me and you.

Moms striving hard, just to get a little buck,

When Dads get a little pick, he call it wuk.

For times were hard, dry and brown;

Most weeks papa ain't had a cent to carry town.

Cheap pension pumps and we trodding to school,

We were told to study schoolwork so we won't be no fool.

Those times was a real struggle I can never forget,

Day and night come and we ain't see breakfast yet.

No one would like to go back to those days again,

To go forward is good to remember the pain.

Some people high post now got them feel so great,

They can't help a poor brother for goodness' sake.

In the end we can't take it where we will all go,

Where body goes to earth and spirit just soar.

Part of 'remembering when' is for yourself too,

Reminding us of the tough times, yet we pull through.

So how can I forget the struggles that we have been through,

When granny took care of me and you?

Giving Thanks to the Gods

I will always give thanks to the gods every day,

For by their laws am I living and that's how I will stay.

From all in my youth they have been seeing me through,

And each time I stumble, they make my spirit renew.

As far as I could remember, all I ever seek was the truth:

Why black people are in this position and mouths still on mute?

Some who went university know what I am talking about,

Yet by organisational status have to shut up their mout'.

Although they know it and still ain't helping to open the poor man eyes,

In fact they would rather tell you about that old colonial lie.

You see some of them get what they never had before,

Still plugged in to that colonial way, still knocking at his door.

So by the time they catch themselves, they are all feeling shame,

Trying their best to catch up to that thing called fame.

Seven days and nights with only one thing on their mind,

Its amazing the mentality of so many people are so far behind.

So in these times I do thank the gods for teaching me so well,

And for taking me clear out of that sea of mental financial hell.

So who so ever reads this know that the gods do exist,

And, in truth and in fact, that is no myth.

They are in us around us, all natural, I can say,

Just reach for them, touch them, embrace them, in each and every way.

Awareness

Highest ones, continue to help me fight, the fight of righteousness I must stand,

To win the great war for humanity is yet my desired plan.

This journey is rough; each time I strive to make a clear headway,

Yet onward trodding with face to the sun, of righteousness I must stay.

Despite the road is yet so hard, I know I am not on my own,

You are all with me, we will fight the fight of the bad seeds that mankind has sown.

In the valley ahead what do we see, pure wickedness come to fight us all,

With righteousness and hearts in place we will have to answer that call.

Never look back! We will stand our ground!

Never in this life again will they wear our crown.

No fear at all, for the seal can no longer be moved,

It was written in eternity and will again be proved.

Beliefs

All that you were taught about life and death - how much
do you hold on to?

When the things you think are the truth, how do you know
there are true?

Some live by believing, but what does believing mean?

How many works by believing are really seen?

Some just hold on to most things that have been said,

Believing deep inside, making it their daily bread.

Do you know when one dies, only the physical decays,

Yet the spirit moves on and lives in the same way.

Who I am on the outside is not really me,

Its my shell you are looking at, I am sure some will agree.

That spirit in I you can't really know,

I assure you that's how the cycle of life goes.

The things that you believe - are they really true?

Would you not research them? That is something I would
do.

I always do what I do best, check for the facts over again,

At the end of it, all the truth – and only the truth – will
always remain.

God's Greatness

Can you tell me the word that is greater than 'thanks'?

Then I shall extend it to the highest ones.

Be there such a word, let us search it out as far as from early morn.

It is such a blessing when we call on the gods, who are with us on life journey's way,

It gives great glory to honour our gods with strength in them we'll stay.

There's got to be a word that is better than 'thanks' for all the goodness you have done for us,

So as long as we live we'll find that word for you, that is surely a must.

Oh most gracious and humble ones, how powerfully majestic are your names,

With all my trust I put in you, with you I will always remain.

And at the centre of it all, thou are so great as the east stretches out to the west,

All excellence I have ever known of thee, all truth lays in thy bosom rest.

So tell me that word that is better than 'thanks', teach me such a word in this time,

We honour thee our gods with great preciousness, in thine arms are all divine.

Doing Good

How can I stop from doing good,

To stop doing the things I know I should.

For everyone I meet on my journey's way,

Never will I do wrong, not while I have a say.

My friend, whatever you have given to those in need,

By doing such kindness, you have sown that seed.

Greed is the word when you don't share with no one,

More despair will it bring, that is all that will be drawn.

People, when you do good, only good will return,

And when that happens, even more will we learn.

By this Mother Nature will never leave you out,

When things get real tough, you can still run your route.

What goes around will always come around, for sure,

So, my friends, please keep knocking at righteousness'
door,

By knocking at that door you will end up doing good,

Than you will always do the things that you know you
should.

Expressions of Righteousness

Expressions of righteousness blooming sweet from early morn,

Sweet expressions of righteousness glowing from dusk till dawn.

With it comes a little for you and a little for me,

It's all around us, why can't you see?

Why try to escape it for its all in our way,

Amazingly it sometimes show itself in the little things we do and say.

Apply expressions of righteousness in everything you do,

And I assure you sooner or later, your reality's dreams will come true.

When trials and troubles come to fight you along life's way,

Let expressions of righteousness guide you as you go to pray.

Just humble yourself for it will come sooner than you think,

Let not the bad ways of life take you to the brink.

Some of us have been there and our lives came very close,

Far from that many people have already given up the ghost.

Yet by pure expressions of righteousness we can all look back,

Then all righteousness will welcome us and that is a true fact.

Natural Rhythms

Deep Down In De Dirt

Early in de morning, before de sun could rise,

I up wid me tools and I looking fa me prize.

Straight across de pasture and down de hill,

While most people only sleeping still.

Down in de dirt is de place to be,

When I down there, I feeling so irie.[3]

In de middle of nature sweet living all around,

Even the birds and bees making they sweet sound.

While de works going on I am enjoying much toil,

Forking and hoeing down in de soil.

I wukking real hard and getting a good sweat,

Wid sweet breeze blowing through, I ain't feeling nutten yet.

Dat is one of de sweetest times to work;

Dis is de place to be, deep down in de dirt.

Some may think this job is really hard to do,

But when I reap the food, they would get some too.

And by de time de sun come up, I got she looking real sweet,

Beds dun mek up and everything looking neat.

Seeds dun plant and I waiting fa dem rains,

Boy when dat come it relieves all other pains.

---

[3] Irie – Jamaican patois meaning 'feeling fine/alright/blessed.

Talk about de bananas, plantains and figs, if ya please,

So much food 'bout here, don't feel nuh squeeze.

This is some of de hard work from this man,

Sweet potatoes, pumpkin, and even some yam.

Oh what a joy this man have behold,

I love this wuk right here deep down in de mould.

Expressions of Beauty

Expressions of beauty upon a crystal night,

Raining musicians upon my ears with loving friends on sight.

Which can only be found in the picturing gloom,

Never in the concrete, always under the bright lit moon.

Pure expressions of beauty hidden in the twilight zone,

Dancing candles in the sky of light, where each one has a home.

Where darkness never hides its face,

Such glittering lights, each holds their space.

Each night is where these beauties all meet,

We enjoy it all; oh, what a treat!

It's a sweet joy and a beautiful sight to see,

Pure expressions of beauty – please, come join me!

Nature

When nature calls out to us all, what will some people do?

It comes in every form at us even where the four winds blew.

I love to hear the birds and bees and whatever is flying by,

Or see the sun on the morning grass as she glitters and rises so high,

So much sweet joy with the rising sun, such beauty to behold,

When rainbow touches sky and sea the glory of God unfolds.

Let's watch the moon as she flies so high, deep within the crystal night,

Where joy of ladybirds do sway, completing the glittering light.

Have you watched the birds that sing so high,

Or the flock of them all as they passes by?

Oh how they fly and sing their sweet tune,

All across the silver-lit moon!

By next evening, all quietly comes to a rest,

After a long day's journey, they have given their best.

From that tiny ant to that huge tree that sways,

When nature calls, she always has her ways.

Mother Nature

Sunshine bursting through thick clouds early morn,

So peaceful, so graceful, like the great silent dawn.

Drawn grey bliss from beautiful horizon set,

Raining melodies of water one can never forget.

This glamour is called the southeast rain,

Blasting hard on the seas again and again.

A whole different scene on the northeast bound,

With a precious cool breeze that wears the morning crown.

Yet the blueness of the sky won't even fade;

Sunshine presses through ocean clouds, perfect picture made.

All for eyes to see as the brightness rose,

Such excellent beauty where all nature grows.

It starts early in the morning, where the sun will always rise,

When nature comes together with all different cries.

Cries of joy of creatures great and small,

Sounds of Creation, sounds of life; the sun sees them all.

How much greater when seen or heard can this all be,

When Mother Nature calls out to you and me?

With Rainbow colours of peace far beyond sight,

Pure sounds of love glazing through crystal light.

So, friends, it's time to rise and watch how nature flows,

Each time we do it, we get stronger as we continue to grow.

Sounds of Nature

Wow, just listen carefully to the breeze that's blowing through the leaves,

How sweet is the sound of the wonderful voices of those lovely little bees.

Nature is calling! How can we all tell,

Birds sweetly singing! just listen and listen well.

We sit and meditate on them all,

Sweet sounds of life as we hear each call.

All unique with their sweet, different sounds,

So peaceful, so graceful in their delicate crowns.

One can gain so much when one listens to their beat,

The sounds each one brings makes one feel complete.

They are singing melodies from dusk until dawn,

Soaking in their rhythm as far as early morn.

We can only hear them when we listen carefully,

They all make up Nature, I am sure we all can agree!

Our Springs

Oh what a beautiful place to be, in our wonderful island springs;

Where peace, love and laughter abide, such joy to all nature brings.

Such elegant peace each one just brings sweet majesty all about,

Makes one meditate on nature at work helps to let the frustration out.

Waters flowing from deep beneath God's earth,

Filtering through layers of limestone, giving her crystals worth.

These springs have real significance to us all, they are where our ancestors came,

To renew their strength from the battering of their faces and the hardships of life's pain.

One should always respect the few that are still left,

For all the rest were stopped, yet we are still blessed.

At these springs we will truly find purity and tranquillity,

Just look for it, open your eyes, and I know you shall surely see.

With viewpoints one can see ocean blue,

Spectacular landscapes, both sea and sky, where sweet nature grew.

These springs do bring a great peace to us all.

Where we hear the cries of our ancestors' call,

So lets cherish and try to keep the waters pure,

With humbleness of hearts our love will forever endure.

Doves Cooing

Let's listen to those little doves coo,

Making sweet melodies just for me and you.

From a distance one can hear their delicate call,

Playing music so sweetly just for one and all.

Some superstitious people say that is death knocking at you,

But if that was so, everyone would be dead too!

Almost in every tree one can hear a dove cooing every day,

Making sweet melodies in their own special way.

Not another sound around you can hear like that,

Landing on your housetop you can hear them chat.

"That's how they all mate," one man would say,

So peaceful, so divine, I love them all the way.

Whenever you hear them just listen to their coo,

It carries a unique special beat, like the wind blowing through.

So delicate to one's ears whenever we hear,

Our sweet earthly doves; their sounds forever we will care.

Reef warriors

What a serious task it must be when one risks their life out on that reef,

So much a story stretching from shore to sand even with that green grape leaf.

One must be brave to do what we do when we battle those currents every day,

Just to school ours and feed ourselves we fight the battle in every way.

Some think it's easy; I dare say not! One could meet dangers at anytime,

From that razor teeth barracuda to that slippery eel, who you can always find.

Even manawars[4] - them stinging jellyfish - one have to keep they eyes peel.

Concentration is the very key, for in an instant you can be a meal.

The reef is only for the brave in heart, so when you can't take it say no,

The simplest error can take you away deep where the channels do flow.

It reminds me of a soldier going out to fight,

He fought so hard, he fought with all his might.

Yet it's all about who will get back home whole,

So to fight this sea battle you have to be bold.

---

[4] Manawars- man o'wars – poisonous jellyfish with a very painful sting.

Bold as a tiger shark ready to attack,

Teeth like razors with barnacles on its back.

One has to be fierce and never back down,

Always stand firm and ready to defend your crown.

So my tribute is to everyone who combs those seas,

With the determination to feed their families.

We all have to give thanks for the risk we take every day,

To provide for ourselves and our families; for now, that is
how life stay.

Natural Living

I would rather live with nature, with which I surround –

The birds, bees, and wind; oh what a beautiful sound!

Radio or TV could never replace these sweet songs for I,

I choose to live this way, up to the day I die.

Just listen to the wind just blowing through the leaves,

So relaxing, so peaceful, it keeps one's mind at ease.

With all that's going on around us, one needs to meditate,

Not bombarded by unnatural sounds with sometimes negative debate.

I may sound a little old-timish, but that is just how I feel;

My way is to live more natural, by that get less unnatural ordeal.

With truth and fact I will try to live by,

All other negatives from me please just fly!

It's not good to live a life of false and pretence every day,

Do all the good you can for in naturalness someday it will pay.

Litter Bug

What is it about nature that you really know:

When you throw that garbage in the bush, where does it really go?

Every time we do these things, we know it is sadly wrong,

And at the end of it all you are just playing the litterbug song.

People that throw garbage only go and block up our watercourse,

Why contaminate our water when it is our true source?

Can some people see the damage they do when there throw that bottle in the drain?

Just passed two, three garbage cans and acting like they ain't got no brain.

All of those water tunnels we got underground somewhere will cause an overflow,

And when this happens all around you the smell makes you angry – ain't that so?

We got to be realistic and understand, wherever you are, keep it clean.

Do not leave yours clean and dirty someone else, to me that is very mean!

Little boy, keep that snack bag in your pocket until you get to a bin,

Don't throw it on the ground, that's not so nice, it only have Mother Nature suffering!

So again my people when you eat that food, please throw the empties in the garbage can.

When everyone does this everywhere, then with pride and industry we will all stand!

Nature's Rains

Oh Mother Nature I give you thanks for the blessings you have given to I[5],

That sweet great blessing that just came down way up from out of the sky.

What a joy to see it come down so boldly and even yet so fierce,

Soaking the earth with its tender love, so precious we all can embrace.

Without her, though, where would we be? We would suffer badly with thirst and drought,

So when some say, "Rain, go away!", we would die without her, and that is no doubt.

Always love Mother Nature for what she brings – rains, sunshine, storms or dew,

For every time the recycling comes it makes the earth renew.

And without her now how do we get our food crops grow?

It would set us back with lesser food, and that you probably know!

She is a true source that helps us all and with grace gives us strength to live,

Precious commodity whenever she rains, pure vitality she always gives.

---

[5] 'I' replaces 'me' in Rastafarian speech. Iyaric – Dread Talk, https://en.wikipedia.org/wiki/Iyaric

So, Mother Nature, I give you thanks for the great blessings you have given to us all,

Great energy we draw from you each time, just as we heed your call.

Mother Nature I

Oh, Mother Nature, I give thanks to thee,

For your guidance and protection for allowing me to see;

Of your sweet love I will always be blessed,

Laying always in your bosom is your slumbering rest.

There are so many times that we hear your call,

Yet most of the times never answer at all.

Some have ears yet cannot hear your sound,

Which rings nonstop, for it's all around.

Both day and night we do hear your voice;

To hear you well yet is still one's choice.

Of your great stories many have been told,

Yet the swiftness of your nature does sometimes act bold.

With all of your stern warnings mankind sometimes does regret,

And of your ruthlessness no one can ever forget.

Still Mother Nature you are kind at your very best,

Peaceful and loving blending 'majesticness'.

So much great things we can yet speak of you,

Wherever we are, you, Mother Nature – you are always true!

Modern-Day Rhythms

The Struggle

There was a time in our lives we could never
forget,

Mom and dad still wukking from sunrise till sunset.

Why is it so some don't really know,

We have to struggle hard after the seeds that massa
sow.

Some are still wondering how this came to be,

They forgot we were bought and sold in their
slavery.

All of this every black person should know,

Back then was only work, that's how we all grow.

Some of us grow to know the truth within,

And to find oneself in life seems so grim.

That great family stability is what we all lost,

Long time ago as we were taken from the north.

A system that was set in place,

That our children's children would be disgraced.

All polished up in what we call a week's salary,

To make us all feel that we are free.

But his story is what we all got,

And our story our children know not.

So we will teach them the ways that justice stands
for all,

That equal rights and justice will never fall.

For the days will come we will regain our strength,

The strength of our ancestors before the first ship
was sent.

How Many More Tears

How many more tears must I cry,

When so many of us are still living a lie?

In a system that breaks you to comply,

Even for the rights that we live by.

A hold lot of people have crumbled; all fall,

Yet there are those who want it all.

A life of greed, that's what we were taught,

To harm one another, that's what we sought.

So many of us have been deceived,

By following those that we believe.

Never taking the time to know the truth,

That will set you free, that is our proof.

Every time I hear my ancestors call,

I feel so hurt, I stumble and fall.

A pain that will never ever stop,

As they bend their backs hard to cut his crop.

To do such to a race that have done them no
wrong,

We were only living our lives as the days move along.

Some may ask what really happened back then,

But the truth will reveal itself, my friend.

Just seek for yourself and no longer fall for their lie,

And when you know, maybe you will sit and cry.

Cry tears of never-ending sadness

In this evil that they have created – a world of madness!

Don't be fooled; money is at the root of it all,

So be careful when you go to answer that call.

Money Lovers

There was a time when I wondered why people
were bought and sold,

How stories that we often heard come so far so
cold.

It's a lot to do with money – you know what
people do with it,

To buy all the things that money can buy, even the
slavery's bit.

How sad the things that money can do to put great
people in chains,

To make one feel less than they are just to satisfy
one's gain.

Funny, we never started with that, for money was
not our way,

We would trade with one another so well and that's
how we would pay.

People fall in love with this thing called money,
never knowing how it came to be,

To fantasise in it to enslave the mind, most of the
time you see.

Mankind has lost his way with it as far as who
knows when,

The greed that comes along with it bring scars that

never mend.

The things that people would do for it just to make a very fast buck,

The degradation of life itself just ends one in the muck.

Money has destroyed so many lives from the time it began until now,

The power that people carry with it causes lots of ones to bow.

One must learn always to conquer this – never let it take your mind,

Be smart and overcome this thing so you'll never be left behind.

Anytime it can control you,

You can lose your soul – and that is so true.

How Far Did We Come from?

How far did we come from? Have you ever really thought,

What was the distance we came from, how we were sold and bought.

We have journeyed through time and space from the deepest places yet,

Never on a journey's haste in a zone where time and space set.

How far did we really come from? As far as east goes to the west,

Where matter is the universe stars in they never ending vastness.

Of all the stories that they have told, which one can we say is truth,

In the way that we were bought and sold the scars do carry the proof.

How sad to enslave a people and don't know where they are from,

Not knowing that the place we came from is where all life begun.

Further than the deepest deep,

Far in the galaxy did the black man leap.

So how far did we all come from? Our oppressors can never know,

Take oneself beyond the beginning where only time and space do glow.

With all her stars glittering all in gold -

Nut is her name, she carries a thousand souls.

SELF MADE PRISON

How many people have locked themselves deep
within prison walls,

How many people can see it coming – that pride
before a fall?

Some people have eyes yet cannot see the journey
tried and true,

Some lack the vision that takes them forth beyond
the sky so blue.

Those who set up their own mental bars, yet
cannot see it so

Only hurt themselves and others and most times
don't even know.

Those old colonial stories that for them will never
depart,

Stories from way back then — oh, how they rend
my heart!

So why be still locked so deep in chains of things
long past and gone,

For their burdens only hold us back in which eyes
can't see the morn'.

Tradition is not always a bad thing, yet all is not the
truth,

Some live to please and please to live, some live tradition from their youth.

Some things that one will never let go seem easier to be locked within,

Self-made prisons are all around; they make pure joy feel grim.

When one is in their self-made jail, it is indeed a very sad place,

Without the reality of the truth, life can be such a waste.

Not only to self but surely to others who are around,

Far from joy others will see your life will always run aground.

So unlock those doors that seem so real that will forever imprison you,

To remove the bondage from oneself and let that light come through.

Oh How I Wish

Oh how I wish I din had ta fight sa hard just ta get a little crumb,

Hustling out there every day some days ya ain't get none.

Life ain't easy fa de poor man doe, wukking from dusk till dawn,

Wukking hard fa dat dolla just tryin ta get dat corn.

Yes its dat dolla dat every day ya duz break ya back ta get

Me papa wuk till he drop, wa ya ain't see nothing yet!

Boy some a we just have fa be only struggling on,

Sometimes de struggle sa hard some pack up and gone foreign!

Now I ain't saying dat I don't like ta wuk,

For ta live nowadays ya have ta go afta dat buck.

And this ain't nothing ta do wid de school ya went,

Some got degrees and na wuk, can't even see a cent.

Poverty is something dat can hit anyone,

So Mr Big Shot don't look me down wid na scorn.

My job real important, so don't watch me feet,

Without me wukking dat land, you won't get food ta eat.

And ya know some people can't get dat do –

Ta survive in hard times some just won't pull through.

So respect everyone wid them wuk every time

All works have purpose, surely yours and mine.

Pain

Where did this pain come from? I just don't even know,

Dis thing keep hurting me from me hip right down ta me toe!

Boy at me age I just can't understand dis thing,

Pain all ova me body is all I feeling!

When a go ta de dock dem don't know wa wrong,

Dem would give me medication and send me along.

Up til now dem can't find de real source a dis pain,

But every day and night um only driving me insane.

Oh Lord, wa ah ain't know wa ta do next,

Wid me face ben up[6] and ah looking real vex;

All that I can do for now is pray to you, oh Jah,

Please free up this pain and let it selah.

---

[6] Ben up – in this context, face scrunched in anger; grimacing

Reality

What does reality say every day, especially to you and I,

What will we gain when we substitute the truth just for a lie?

It's also sad to know the truth and cannot really say,

When some people who think they know it all walk blindly every day.

Reality is the real version of a story truly told,

Not hiding the truth like his story of when we were bought and sold.

So many things they hid from us for a polish up story of their own,

Still wanting us to accept such with the bad seeds that they have sown.

But in reality we all know its still hard to fully escape those whips,

With their mental bars still holding us down, bound to our very hips.

Being paid after we were done so much harm,

With many of our souls buried deep in their

plantation farm.

Yet though think that they have won so far,

But deep down, many hearts will forever bear that scar.

Long have our ancestors prayed for the day to come:

The reality of the truth with the rhythm of the drum.

So the real story is what we will always seek,

For we are a people who are forever unique.

From the existing chains still of today,

For in love and unity, that's how we will stay.

Clinic Wait

Here at the clinic[7], where we all have to wait,

Trying to see the doc before it's too late.

All sick people here, some like they're falling down,

Some trying to pick themselves up from off the ground.

Sickness is a hard thing, no one can tell when,

And when that time comes, we'll all need a friend.

Not much money in our pockets, that's why we are here

We've all come to get some free health care.

Some people like they're are in a daze with no way out

Just wanting to feel better and that is no doubt.

By the minute, more and more people seem to come,

For when that sickness hit you here is the closest place to run.

What makes us so sick? Some don't even know,

Maybe it's the foods we eat – the ones we don't grow.

[7] Clinic – Polyclinic – free health care provider in Barbados

New commercial foods that are so sweet for your mouth,

Only cheap and no good foods come from the south.

We got to learn to eat more of what we grow,

To stop most sickness stop putting ourselves on death row.

Let us all try to eat right each and every time,

To keep away from clinics and we'll surely feel refined.

Clinic

These days at de clinic got me feeling like hell,

Wid so much sick people – including de smell!

Flies all ova de place lan'ing pun ya where eva ya go,

People walking wid sticks, trodding to and fro.

Ah sa hungry ah feeling weak by now,

This bad feeling, wa I surely can't allow!

Waiting ta see de doc fa nearly a whole day here,

So much pain in me back yet I cannot even share.

Only thing left ta do right now is to wait it out,

And sit and pray fa de doc ta soon come about.

No other choice I seems to have for I ain't got na money,

Got ta wait on this free health care no matter rain or sunny.

Dat Ting Call Wuk

Now early every morning before de sun could come up,

Lots of people wake up to go ta dis ting call wuk.

All ya could hear is de minibuses[8] rolling through,

And most people who get on them face looking screw!

I always know what time it is,

Cause ya got ta come out of ya hole, whether rain or bliss.

Wherever you are and you hear them pass,

Ya betta be on time cause dem always moving fast!

Always remind me of dem old slave ships,

Still in slavery — only leave out de whips.

Dat is de time ya have ta step out,

Looking fa dat dolla every man just run he route.

Don't matter how far ya have ta go fa dis ting,

Every morning pun dem vans pure stress it bringing.

Ya feel sa breakup on ya off day now,

______

[8] Minibus – A type of privately-owned public transportation in Barbados

Can't even help ya self feel like mrs brown old
cow.

By de time ya look round ya back ta work again,

Cause ya want de lil money doe it driving ya insane.

Got ta get pon de people wuk early, ya hear,

Don't get there early and think de boss man care.

When he let ya go someone else will hold de space,

He said, "Easy come easy go, don't watch na
face[9]."

I could go on and on, but I will stop here for now,

Killing me self behind people wuk will I not allow.

Let me be self employed right down ta de end,

Mek me feel sa fine[10]; for she is a god send.

____

[9] "Don't watch na face." – Bajan slang for 'don't worry about it.'
[10] "Mek ma feel sa fine" – Bajan slang for 'Makes me feel so happy'

Over Time

Evening come and I like I can't stop wuk,

'Ova time' dem call it, and I can't even duck.

Ya mean afta I nearly kill meself all day,

When its time ta ga home, boss man start ta bray.

He says, "Ya could put in another two hours, ya know,"

And I'm getting real vex, but I can't let it show.

All he is interested in is he wuk getting done,

After I wuk sa hard in de boiling sun.

This is de price ya have fa pay when ya wuk fa dem man,

Even de lil ova time ya wuk fa tax man jucking in he hand.

But somehow ya tryin ta mek de boss feel pleased,

In reality ma back really need a little ease.

So when de evening come please let me go,

Cause when I get home of dat wuk even more.

Its call home work now if ya please,

But in truth and fact ma body need an ease.

All evening til night I still pun de move,

Now tell me when do I step out of dis wuk groove.

Unjust People

Its funny how some people live by doing injustice every day,

Always right to themselves and deceitful in every way.

Pretending always to be that good sweet one,

Deriving evil in their hearts as from early morn.

These people never seems to take no blame,

And in their wickedness their carry no shame.

Some of them using Christianity as their tool,

Going to church on Sundays and looking so cool,

But during the week they would only transform,

Ask them for a dollar and they would treat you with scorn.

Some in their big rides would just pass you by,

Now come from in church and still living a lie.

Boy, some people feel that they are all saints,

Far from the truth and minds only taint—

After reading this, don't think that I hate them though,

It's the things they do that makes them look low.

All of this is pure backwardness that I see,

If you ain't true to yourself just let it be.

Abuse

How do we find the joy we seek? How do we bring it out?

It's not in the things we do and say when we just scream and shout,

That's call abuse; that is what I see when we say things that hurt,

It makes you want to run away to wonder what life is worth.

How can we care and say we love and do them wrong all the time?

If someone did the same to us, we think the punishment will fit the crime.

What you don't like for you, don't do to no one — it's sad when you hurt her so,

Why try your best to let her down feel sad when she let you go?

If you don't feel the way you used to its good to tell her the truth,

It's better to tell and not give abuse, for each scar will bear the proof.

So where do we find this joy we seek? It surely ain't in abuse,

Either physical, mental or verbal it's all the same
and comes with great misuse.

Don't fool yourself that is no real love waking up
to that every day,

The heart that knows the truth to seek works it out
in every way.

Have You Ever Wondered?

This thing call money, look how fast it does go,

That little bit you just work for like the wind that just blow –

As soon as you get this thing, it out your hand so fast,

With small amounts like this it surely can't last.

Bills coming at you from left and right,

Can't hide at all though — money gone on strike.

This money thing hard when its coming so small,

Pockets so empty I have to beg for a phone call!

These big shots around here do not even help the poor,

And at election time would come knocking at your door.

Big money tricks around here got man scratching his head,

Dem don't seem to understand that things real dread.

When its time to buy food I can't even get out of the gate,

To tell my girl that it ends up in a long debate.

How to hold down this thing? It like it got wings,

More work and less pay only sadness this brings.

I need to find another way to make some more,

To stop this thing call poverty from knocking at my door.

And to think about it surely it can leave you in a mess,

Having a little or plenty can bring you pure stress.

It is designed to play with your mind – it's true,

Don't know yourself and it can even trick you.

Its not easy to wake up and think money every day,

One thing for sure – bills will never go away.

If we try to help each other with the little we have got,

Maybe someday in return you will get a whole lot.

So don't try to hold to it with all your might,

Help up your little brother or sister, for you know it's right.

Last Day of 2015

Last day of the year! The winds are blowing so strong,

Winds are so hard they want to blow you down.

Seas rough with white caps streaming all across,

Birds high in the sky never seem to be lost.

Some would say it was a good year for them,

For throughout the year bad fences were on the mend.

Some others can't say the same for themselves,

Poor man still struggling while rich man grabbling after the wealth.

It was another challenging year for I all the way,

I still end up with the same issues I started with the first day.

I would not say financially I had a very good one,

I didn't make a lot of money, yet I still held on.

So last day of the year winds just blow on with haste,

Show yourself, oh precious wind, as we feel your grace!

Dis Money Ting

Dis thing without wings look how fast it does fly,

De more ya get a dis ting de fasta it say goodbye.

This ting dat we think dat we know so much about,

Got most people thinking dat DEM cannot do without.

Pure monopoly keep playing wid de poor people's head,

Robbing us all the time and don't care if we dead!

From as early as a youth learning tuh spend dis thing,

Give me a little allowance and ya could mek me sing!

Not teaching us of the reality of every dime,

If ya love it too much ya could end up doing crime.

Dat is what will happen if ya don't teach dem de right way,

They would go through life getting trick every day.

Let's be real and always show dem the truth,

And always remember you were also a youth.

By doing this how to deal with money each one will know

How ta truly balance themselves that their money can grow.

Money, Money, Money

I could neva come ta like this thing,

From de first money dat come about, pure stress dat bring.

To study de man dat got a lot he ain't want ta fall from there,

For when he fall he'll hit sa hard only shame face all de way

Yet he will try to get more by enslaving me and you,

With more deceit and more evil in his ungrateful brew.

Before running afta dis money please stop and check ya self,

What is your motive for getting so much — for helping or only fa wealth?

With bills coming from left ta right,

Most weeks man cant see a dolla pun sight!

So does it matter if ya rich or poor?

Both of dem will bring stress galore!

Ya see both of dem have ta go after it,

At all costs to mek ya feel like ya benefit.

So dis whole money scam is a big lie fa I,

There have ta use our hands ta get their money fly.

Without our hands there will all be no more,

And slaving fa dem would be dun wid for sure.

All ya need ta know bout this money is how ta deal wid it,

And in de end I am sure all the pieces of the puzzle will finally fit.

A Long Short Story

There would love us to forget what their ancestors did to ours,

But for all eternity we will carry our sorrows.

Still some have forgiven and are learning to let go,

Yet some are acting like it was never really so.

Many things that were done, many stories are untold,

Some so painful and traumatic one would only turn cold.

We have survived the great slaughter for the money they have earned,

Now the greatest question to ask is what we have really learned.

Lots of us have learned to be like them in their money game,

Trampling on others to get to the top, now isn't that a shame?

Now is that the only way that you were taught –

To do even worse than them, is this what you sought?

Old folks said day runs until night catch up with it,

Who continue to do wickedness, someday bound to quit.

All things that have a beginning must come to an end,

Including those of us who have no heart — you too, my friend!

Running down Money

Tell me why must I run down money every day,

Just to know shortly it will turn and fly away?

This thing that most people put all their trust in,

After doing anything for it, on their face there is no grin.

You see the white man printed this thing a long time ago,

And with greed he kept printing to make his money bank grow.

Yet check the mental state it has poor people's minds in,

Psychological and financial – got poor people scrambling.

Don't talk about financial, when you have to make ends meet,

And at the end of it all, some still end up in the street.

You see, most of us never took time to study this mock thing,

We got tricked so much poor people only got the stress that it bring.

Imagine granny use to work for two shillings a week,

While massa raking in the millions from her hands and feeling sweet.

And she feels good for that can add some food to her supply,

And after that not a cent she can save, for the rest said "Buy, buy!"

Now Monday come and she have to start all over again,

Could hardly find five cents like it playing with she brain.

This money have so much stress you have to put up with,

People, the reality is money a big myth.

So I ask myself why must I run down money every day?

To prove what? So that I can get pay?

Tender for whatever services I have done,

Life never began so, no not under the sun.

Looking Within

How much time do you get to look within,

And how important is it to you to find that castle in your skin?

When we continue to look to God only true love will we give,

From day to night as we commit ourselves from the beginning so we can live.

Taking time out to look within is one of the keys to life's success,

It gives one time to make conscious moves to do your very best.

This whole money business on people's mind taught us to be always on the go,

Could hardly get time to check oneself, yet so much we don't really know.

Why do we have to keep pushing ourselves both day and night,

And at the end your body is saying, "Something just ain't right?"

It's like you have to run down that dollar until you drop down dead,

With no knowledge of who you are and still the money urge has to be fed.

We need the food of righteousness to truly sustain life,

Instead, we get overworked and underpaid yet we make the sacrifice.

So taking time to look within is not such a bad thing to do,

It helps you to clear your mind with whatever you are going through.

Classes

What makes you feel that you are better than I?

Is it the big car you drive or the things that you can buy?

It's amazing how material things make you look down on me so,

And with my patchy clothes you judge me from head to toe.

So it's money that makes you feel that you are in a class,

And you forget where you came from while you put on that mask.

You've moved into the heights and feel like a big shot now,

Treating people how you like, that's how low you have bowed.

My friend, class is just a phase that you are going through,

When material make you feel that you are better than me - then who is fooling who?

When you climb that tree so high, make sure you do not fall,

For those poor folks that you treated so bad don't hear your call.

Who ever climbs the highest will hit harder when they land,

Always check yourself up there or your life will be like sinking sand.

Boss man, material could never make me feel that I am better than you,

It has been proven already and I can prove it again, too —

Which man has ever said that class did save his life,

If that was so, then death would be no strife.

Now it's time to go and you can't carry class with you,

The same people that you let down you, wish would help pull you through.

While your breath has slowly began to slip away,

You are now remembering all the bad things you did and everything you shouldn't say.

How you have let down your good friend that you have grown up with,

Look how money and class make you treat that poor kid.

It does not matter how much I have I know better than that,

I don't have to be in no class, I would rather stay flat.

Guns

Now where are all of these guns coming from in
our small island called Bim?

I am sure it can't be the small fish that are bringing
them in!

Big shots out here! When cargo touch down no
one will ever search them

Bringing in all of the latest weapons every time
'cause they got their big shot friend.

You see more money is the thing that always seems
to bring more greed to their hearts,

So while selling their souls they surely think their
money will never depart.

They are only helping to enable poor people to kill
each other slow,

For these guns do end up in poor people's hands
and that ain't no pappy show.

So the minds of plenty people ain't got nothing in
it,

Their food is Bustas[11] and rock cakes – that's why
crime is so easy to commit!

____

[11] Busta – a brand of soft drink

While the big men who are selling the guns are still selling them every day,

Watching the news of how many people are getting shot and still ain't care

Money stash away good and showing no sympathy still,

Mind so dark and tainted, always on their money thrill!

What We Were Taught

What a big massa lie:

Ecless.10:19: 'a feast is made for laughter and wine maketh merry; but money answer all things.'

Listen to the big massa lie that money is the answer to everything!

For with that money they say so much joy it can bring,

He carefully studies how to further enslave us,

By printing some dollars to make man feel famous.

Fresh dollar notes — oh Lord: this money smell brand new,

So much things on your mind and still wondering what to do.

The trick is his mock money is giving him even more power to succeed,

Causing more destruction on his quest for more while on his money creed.

Some of our own minds have become masters of tricks with this thing,

Never caring about the pain and suffering to some that it bring.

When you become dependant on it and can hardly see a cent,

With food to buy and bills to pay now where will your frustration vent?

And on top of that, everything somehow is highly taxed,

In reality it's only grinding poor people to the max!

Unfortunately when you say D you have to also say B,

A whole lot of us are still following the massa trend, you see.

Good people get money and seem to forget where there came from,

That money gone to their head so no one else can get none.

From their mother who born them they ain't giving a cent to,

Still you forget the years that mommy nurture and feed you.

That piece of land granny died and leave you suddenly want all now,

Playing the same greedy massa game for, that is how low you have bowed.

You were never taught to use the money to help build one another,

Letting it control your mind to even deny your own brother.

These same tricks massa played on us we are now playing them on ourselves,

By denying those who are desperately in need while running after your wealth.

Have you ever stopped and asked yourself why some people are this way,

It all finds itself in the greed of that money and that's all I have to say!

Gran Son

Look what that boy cause that money to make him do,

The damage he had done I don't think he has a clue.

Born and grew up at gran for most of his life,

Mother live there too and would always make the sacrifice.

This boy was the joy of the old folks at the time,

Grew up to be a man and everything was so fine.

When big sis got sick Mr man started to disappear,

Down by his father like he ain't really care.

Big sis pass on now, oh how sad for us all,

We all knew that someday we would have to answer that call.

Sis dead and gone yet leave some money on the bank,

Mom and dad's names were down and big sis was very frank.

In these tough economic times every cent would count,

Things so hard on poor people it does not matter
the amount.

I witness tears run down from my old girl eyes,

The man drew off every cent by using false lies.

These old folks TV is off because they ain't get the
bills pay,

Getting pension once a month for government
don't seem to care.

Taxes triple up and things real rough,

How could he do such to the old folks knowing
that things tough?

The old people always say what you sow one day
you will surely reap,

So when karma fall on some people, my silence I
will keep.

How could he leave his grans sitting out in the cold

While he took all the money? I watch as the
scenario unfold.

Look how sad a little money can cause one to lose
their dignity,

And all of the sense you have to look into yourself
you cant see!

Some people in life will remain blind even until
their end,

He suddenly forget the things gran did and on him
the money they spend —

For mom didn't do all for him, grans did some too,
that's why they would hurt,

This sometimes causes one to question themselves,
to wonder what life's worth.

People do these things thinking that they will
answer at no time at all,

Yet will look to the same ones they hurt each time
they stumble and fall.

Everything we do including the wrong will one day
haunt us to our grave,

When you disrespect our elders who cared for us
so much your life you cannot even save.

Poor People's Voices

Where are poor people's voices being heard? Can anyone tell me where?

When injustice is done to the poor, is there anyone that really cares?

Delinquent families still all over this land, it doesn't take a scholar to realise that,

Dating all the way back from slavery, now isn't that a true fact?

For poor people's voices, nothing much has changed in this rock we call Bim,

For the minds of our leaders are tainted by money, grabbing as much as they can skim.

It's a shame when poor people have no voice, no matter where they are in this world,

All the plans to keep poor people down – it's like real caring has taken a swirl.

Some of us know what is going on for our modern day massas running this thing,

With great burdens they lay on poor people's backs, only more stress does this bring.

We are the silent lambs who have no say in this political polish-up world,

With inflation so high and things so tight many days would just sit and curl.

Seriously, where are the voices of poor people being heard – in the country or in the town?

Only a poor man they would sell a cheap gun, justifying it, knowing it is wrong!

A lot of untrained minds and no proper food, how will they expect them to think?

With so many minds lost so far away no wonder some live life on the brink.

Tell me, how much more injustices can poor people take?

With no voices at all and that is not no debate.

Poor people fall short at the mercy of the rich,

So poor man, please be wise and don't you ever switch!

Money Effect

The day you do not have money, how does that affect you?

every day you are looking hard for a job and there ain't nothing to do.

Do not even know how to get the next bill pay,

Children going to school hungry, this happening almost every day.

Look what this little rock come to! Poor people out here suffering bad,

While government talking millions! For poor people, that got to be sad.

But when it goes like this, it is not so hard to get addicted to this thing,

Some never know the pain one goes through only see the joy that money can bring.

That's why so many have fallen victim to this thing called money, you see,

Thinking its the best thing that ever happen to them, oh now isn't that funny!

With pure deception at the base of it all,

Many take many lengths just to answer that call.

That day you don't have the money, what's really running through your mind?

With so much to do and so little to go by, questioning yourself every time.

Some just pretend it's OK, yet some will never swallow that,

While some can put plenty food on their tables and other's bellies are only flat.

Now think about it, that day you don't have money, how will that affect you?

Think about it again and again… that is what most poor people go through.

Keys

Whatsoever we are going through in life,
endurance is one of the keys,

So many obstacles from all around can bring you
down to your knees.

Most times life is so hard you feel like you just
want to give up,

And that ever winding road that's always so tough
makes it harder to fill that cup.

Then that little voice says to you, "Don't you ever
give up, please don't ever let go,

Endure this thing a little longer despite the journey
seems slow."

For most poor people this journey seems to
become harder most of the time,

Yet with love and patience in your heart, one day it
will work out fine.

With righteousness as one of your keys, I am sure
you will never fail,

Doesn't matter how hard it gets, my friend, hold
on and balance that scale.

These are sure keys that we can hold onto in life
when times get rough,

Mix them together and use them wisely to remove some of the sad stuff.

It doesn't matter who you are in this world, obstacles will come your way,

It's how you address each and every one that will prove your endurance every day.

Curious George

There is no one as curious as that man call George
every time we go down to the beach,

The only one who would travel the world and want
to know everything before he reach!

That man named George will ask you a thousand
questions about each and everything,

Sometimes he gets so personal you wonder if its
Hollywood here shooting a film!

George want to know from where you went to
school to even where you were born,

It does not matter where you came from, could be
from Bim or from foreign.

Mr. George will ask you questions from start until
end,

Then he will want to take your picture and call you
his friend.

There is not a time I go to the beach and he is not
there,

It's like he needs to always know about us; what he
needs to know still we ain't clear!

They studied us a long time ago and know more
about us than we could ever think,

Maybe after doing us so much wrong singing that money song,

Believing their ship will never sink!

Money Control

Why must I allow money to determine my walk?

And why will I allow it to control my thought?

We have all seen what it has done to the poor,

After loving it so much then to see it no more.

Pure discomfort and stress only dwells on the poor man's mind,

Then to find yourself within it all that you surely cannot find.

Thank the gods for righteousness, for that tells us when we are wrong,

While some of us ignore these same sayings just to sing that money song.

Working twenty-four hours in a day plus seven days a week,

Not far from that you start to feel lost and your life begin to look bleak.

For you are fully plugged in now and putting in your all,

Trying your best to answer that every day money call.

Sometimes you gather up a sum and don't know

what to do with it,

There are so much things you need and still not enough — one could catch a fit!

Just to show all the things that this money make people go through,

Imagine some people are thinking that God made this money for me and you.

I would say it's a shame for mankind to even think this way,

As far as money is concerned, God never brought it here.

God or the gods were never printers of this money you see,

And then why would god make money for humans to be sold in slavery?

Gold, silver, diamonds by the gods were beautifully made,

Not money that came from mankind's heart just to make his own pay grade.

So, again my friend, why must I allow money to determine my walk?

No longer will I be fooled by it for it to control my what I sought.

Think It Through

Youngster, from the time that you think about taking up that gun,

Think carefully of just how your life will then run.

Then, after, picture yourself behind those prison bars,

With not a clue how to heal your mental scars.

Yet, in truth and fact, you are only living a lie,

That is how easy your life will go sailing by.

You think only that man that you killed is dead,

Have you thought, when you are locked up, how your children will be fed?

It is always time to think before you commit that act,

Especially when you end up in jail – and that is a true fact.

You know that moms and your little baby are depending on you,

The only one holding down a little work just to get them through.

Things real tight, yes, but you can't let them down,

How will you feel when they wake up and daddy is not around?

Think carefully before you pull that trigger, friend, for both families will end up with a loss,

With one man dead and the other in jail – that is what not thinking will cost.

Your freedom gone with few privileges – now, how does that make you feel?

You sit in prison for the next 25 years in your mind replaying the whole ordeal.

Only if you could go back in time! What would do different then?

What you did to that man you did to yourself, for to yourself you can't pretend.

Now look what happened to both of them, now their children can't enjoy their smile –

With one man dead and the other having a long time to think, for he will be locked up for a while.

THIS IS WHAT NOT THINKING IT THROUGH WILL COST YOU.

Why the Rush?

Have you ever asked yourself this thing,

When we rush so much, what do we bring?

For sure, it can never be nothing sweet,

Before we could sit down, always fast on our feet.

It is plain enough for all to see,

Rushing gets you nowhere in a big hurry.

Even the ones who have plenty still don't know,

It's just a part of life that should never be so.

Let us take a deep long look at it all,

Rush yourself every day to answer that money's call.

All of the hustling and bustling that you do so much,

Could never be God's way, for God never did such.

Just as we shut our eyes at night,

Before we could rest good it is morning light.

Still want sleep from the night before;

Got to rush again, fast out that door.

The job now takes top priority,

And now have no time for your own family.

No it's not easy at all in this life,

I guess someone has to make that sacrifice.

Now rushing myself to me makes no sense,

Then through it all its only false pretence.

Its killing me slowly and I am feeling the pain,

All of this rushing and rushing will soon drive me insane.

Last Day of 2018

Last day of 2018, oh another year will soon pass by,

Still we have many unanswered questions, wondering why, why, why?

Why there is so much hardship in our dear land,

Still, most poor people's lives are like sinking sand.

People are trying to hold out though prices are on the rise,

While at night and day all we hear is poor peoples cries.

"What a year," most can say – in a few hours it will be gone,

While some people are still trying to get a meal as far as early morn.

Yet, sad as it seems, it is the real truth,

Let's take a walk down to the slums and I will show you the proof.

Frustration

Never let that money take over your mind,

Have or don't have, everything will be fine.

You can always tell when some people pockets brek,

Every little thing that arrive they just start ta fret.

Na money ta buy nothing boy, and their face looking screw,

Ask them what is wrong with them and they want ta beat you.

Ever denying de fact that broke pockets got them sa hot,

Especially when others living so sweet and a cent da ain't even got.

Brother, don't let it get ta ya head; I know what that feels like,

Working sa hard in de boiling sun and on pay day money gone pun flight.

This thing moving fast from ya like it was made ta fly,

For all of de hard work ya put in de money just saying bye-bye…

You see being dependent on this thing could leave
ya in a bad state,

Mentally it could slow ya down and like a balloon
your head could inflate.

People stop denying de truth and see money for
what it is,

Some love this money more than themselves so
their lives will always be a bliss.

So when you have no money at all please don't let
it get you down,

Just remember you may not have none today yet at
some time it will come around.

Cry of the Poor

It's amazing how we poor people do live,

Finding it hard every day and still could always give.

Times so hard and we are still struggling on,

With money running things, before it come, it gone!

Days I don't have a cent to send school my sons,

Cannot even see a bread, 'cause they ain't no funds.

Imagine all the money in the world and people still suffering,

Some governments rather buy arms and leave poor people wondering.

They call it 'recession' in the world, wherever we turn,

Man only draw back is his mock money he print – how much have we learned?

That slippery money wall, how high have you scaled?

No wonder why some people give up: before they start, they fail.

For months now some people ain't see a bag of
rice,

Hard or soft still most of us have to make that
sacrifice.

Still deep in my heart of love I will never let go,

Whatever position I find myself in, only love will I
always sow.

Christmas 2018

Christmas 2018 is right here wid we,

All of the excitement and poor people still in poverty.

Man, woman and child with speed on de go,

And most minds on Christmas with the seeds dem people sow.

That little bit of money that ya save up for de year,

Will obviously be spent and that is so clear.

So much things to buy around this time,

Your mind on that money and that money on ya mind.

Some doing odd jobs here there and all around,

Trying ta keep in tune with that mock Santa clown.

It's amazing how these people still playing tricks with your mind,

For Christmas started with massa, and that was their sign.

We watch and serve carefully especially on that very day,

With nothing in our bellies and not a word we
could say.

We saw them giving each other gifts at a Christmas
we knew nothing about,

Then later on some where in us this Christmas
thing started to sprout.

Amazingly, giving gifts when we were back home
was an every day thing for us all,

So for us every day was a Christmas then, without
answering that money call.

Reaching Out

I would never give up on anyone who is hooked,

Whatever he or she is suffering from I could never close that book.

The reality is had they known before,

Indeed they would have never walk through that door.

Some have done what some would say sadly was the worst,

Just living life on the edge like its a bad curse.

To be in such a place in life, who would like to be,

And every time one catch themselves, their life only feels empty.

Just remember, anyone of your family members this could happen to,

So don't let them down to make that difference, they are surely counting on you.

Just to be understanding with all of the errors that they have made,

Despite some of the unpleasant memories that never seem to fade.

No sense condemning now, for the damage is already done,

We must help them to help themselves for their recovery journey has just begun.

As long as you are real inside you can surely feel their pain,

In the end there will be a maturity of peace that one will always gain.

Learning More

Here I am, an open book, always willing to learn more,

With all my heart all I seek is the truth, as far as righteousness soars.

Every day there is something more to learn, whatever comes your way,

The expressions of every single thing, always has something to say.

Everyone I get in contact with I do learn something from,

Maybe that's my natural gift, who knows? Or maybe it's the Master's plan.

Pick sense from what you think that foolish man say, or the mentally ill man in the street,

You see, everyone has a story to tell; sometimes it's true, though, it may sound bleak.

I take a seat and I listen well as I watch moving things go by,

From that little brown lizard to those tiny ants, even the birds that just fly high.

By listening to learn and learning to listen, I can now write down what I find,

At the end of it all, there is so much to write –
only consciousness flowing through my mind.

Friend, why not try to be an open book, just to
learn something more about life,

To learn more, always set your mind at ease, when
life meets up with strife.

Forgotten Talent

Caribbean people are naturally talented people from birth,

And in truth, some of us know what life is really worth.

Most of us sometimes in life need that little break,

Just to start a real life and to get a little piece of that cake,

And those who are established had to get help from somewhere,

Maybe someone saw their talent and they had that flair.

Now everyone I ask for help never had time to hear a line,

There always referred me to someone else, for that was their only rhyme.

This I find is real sad for some forgot where they came from,

They forget when they first started out, now their help is for only some.

Maybe you have to be a friend of a friend to really get that start,

When deep down inside each and every word
should come clearly from the heart.

In these times it's hard to find someone who is
truly willing to assist,

With so many thoughts coming and so much to
write all naturalness I can't miss.

One thing for sure with all my heart, when I reach
I will always look back,

To help the talented who others don't see – I will
help them, and that's a fact!

There are many out there who are just like me,
have plenty to share with the world,

That service shared in us will forever live and will
always be our joy and pearl.

Untrue Leaders

How many world leaders are about living the
truth? It's like truth don't exist anymore,

Which world leader can you rely on for such truth?
Few seem to be knocking at that door.

Leaders of today live their lives based on lies; boy
this world has truly gone mad,

And with many people backing them up — for
mankind, this is indeed sad.

Most of them keep telling the people bold-faced
lies, even here on the TV,

Calling the motherland a shit-hole place — and his
people just will agree.

They are forgetting the truth and fact that Africa is
still the richest place on earth,

While their ancestors took us from her then called
us slaves — what was that worth?

Now today we need leaders to come clean, from
the pastor all down the line,

Anyone who looks up to you as a leader;
righteousness should be your sign.

You could be a farmer, a painter, whoever you may
be – some will always see leadership in you,

Never deny it, we come from great nobles and
kings! Look into our story and see it's true.

Today it's even harder for the poor to rely on these
leaders who have no place for the truth,

Let us place all our trust in the gods we know; in
them there is always proof.

Imagine billions of dollars in the world today, yet
some people can't even eat,

They want the poor to be at their mercy, to always
have to bow at their feet.

Power and control that's what its called, while
using their money to get it done,

When their time comes will their money save
them? I say no — not under this sun!

ISLAND RHYTHMS

These Shores

These shores of Barbados are no longer free,

Foreign investors buying them up from shore to sea.

When we were small the track we walk to go to the beach,

So surprise! One day I was dumb with speech,

The whole place block up and we can't get back on the beach.

Why the government allowing this? No one seems to know.

Gabby already have a song call 'Jack' – "…don't want me ta bathe on my beach…"

Bajans never know one day on this island this thing could reach.

I am not writing this down just because I feel like,

All Barbadians know this thing can't be right.

Beach called Banana Boat once before was called The Garage,

Errol Barrow, Tom Adams use to go there for time gone, the place was large!

Restaurant and pub out there on the sea, a place

where big shots use to lime,

As a youth passing there going to the sea we always had a good time.

Had someone told me one day my feet will not ever touch that sand,

I would say to them, "No, not in Bim! These things could never stand!"

Oh how wrong I was, for time had gone, yet the same thing come to pass,

Mr Barrow is probably turning over in his grave for his words did not last.

Why do we allow people to buy up beach front and block off every inch,

Making it harder for tourist and Bajan alike to even get a rinse!

Now the whole place we once call Banana Boat block off and we can't get to the sea,

From 'Sand Remo' down to Sandals now privatised; to this I could never agree.

Now I have to walk another half mile just to do my fishing trade,

While the person who bought the land already got it made.

So Barbadians are the fools at the end of it all,

While government only hearing the rich man's call.

What a sad state this place has become —

This land call Barbados, land of the sea and sun.

ZR Squeeze

Now come from wuk and I want to get home quick;

Jump on a ZR[12] and end up feeling sick.

Van nearly full and two big like bull cows sitting in de back,

I gone between them and nearly catch a heart attack.

On de way down de road driver pick up an elephant,

Telling him, 'Guh down in de back!'; to me this sound suh ignorant.

Conductor say, 'Boy, yuh have tuh guh down in dey!'

And I want tuh get home real bad so I ain't got nothing tuh say.

He stuff he down between us wid he face looking mean,

By this time I feel like a little squash sardine.

Squash like a potato every time de van make a rock,

---

[12] ZR – Another (smaller) type of privately owned public transportation system in Barbados; like the *minibus*

And by now feel like a old ben' up fowl-cock.

I said to myself, 'No, this thing cant be fuh me,

I got tuh escape from this before I end up in de
cemetry![13]'

 When I finally get 'way my words was, 'Thank
you, Lord!',

Dem two bull cows and dat elephant nearly brek
me spinal cord.

Sun real hot and yuh feel like ya gine stew,

Man look round and said, "Don't be surprise; dis
ain't nothing new.

Dem accustom ta packing up de van like this,

We pack suh close like we want ta kiss!"

Anyhow, de story took an unexpected twist –

Policeman show up and stop de van,

And ask de conductor, "You think this is a tin can?

Take out some of these people and hold this
report,

Ya won't escape this, 'cause I gine see ya in court!

Boy, wunna must be feel that wunna own de road;

____

[13] Cemetry - cemetery

This ZR pack ta capacity and it fully overload!

Young man, do you know how dangerous that this is?

Anything happen dat insurance with someone's life you will miss!

Never ever let dat dolla make ya a fool,

Cause yuh using people's lives like ya ain't went tuh school.

Fellow, do this thing the way de law say ya should;

It will stop these reports and you will end up feeling good.

So don't ever let me see this thing happening again,

For it is pure madness and people's lives can go down the drain.

Plus de court will take every cent ya mek,

All gine happen in de end you will end up brek!"

Oistins Fish Festival 2018

Oistins Fish Festival is with us here again,

Bring ya family or even a friend.

This is de time you could find all of your treats,

Plenty of things ta buy, plenty of things ta eat.

There got meat down here fuh who like that,

Some love it suh bad they just keep going back!

For those little ones they got plenty of toys on display

All kinds and types buy one, if you may.

Jewellery 'bout here from coral to gold,

All kinds of deals around here and things getting sold.

Clothes? Man wuh? Ya ain't seen nothing yet,

My friend got a stall up here and her name is Bernadette.

This woman got clothes for people all kinds of wear:

Big, small, in between – you name it, boy she got de gear!

Now music and activities? Don't even talk bout them,

Music from top ta bottom like it ain't got nuh end.

Could be a little confusing sometimes as they are so close,

Wa hey - this is de Festival, out of it we have ta mek de most.

Talk bout people! All kinds of people out here in de street,

And don't talk 'bout de girls, all sizes out hay looking real sweet.

Ladies dress up and looking good all in their brand-new suits,

Hair well done, enjoying themselves, some even wearing boots.

Look, ah can't tell ya nuh more! Come – it's a good sight ta see,

Indian, whiteman, chinaman and de Carribean together enjoying festivity.

People, we got tuh keep this thing safe every time it come around,

Nuh violence, nuh badness while we all enjoy de festival song.

I would like tuh stop now, but you know I got a li'l bit more tuh say,

Police got bout hay well lock down, so don't let they be nuh foul play.

That is always a good thing, for things have tuh be safe in de place,

Remember folks, when all is done, everything have tuh always stay safe.

At the Garrison

Horse racing at the Garrison once upon a time,

As youngsters we would say nothing could be so fine.

Times that we all could never forget,

Even to watch the big ones bet.

Plenty of people are there, big and small,

All types of people, short and tall.

Trying to get a blink of the race,

So many people around, we could hardly find a space.

That was a time when there was much fun,

We all loved to run up and down in the burning sun.

Oh how sweet those times truly had been,

With plenty of people here on the scene.

Those were the days we cherish and love so dear,

Money or not, horse racing had that flair.

All grown up now and still loving it so,

Horse racing in these times was like never before.

So why has horse racing lost its flair,

It's like it lost its touch, like it is out of gear.

We don't see lots of people like before,

Wonder what really happened; why it's not exciting anymore?

For that is a mystery only few can tell,

Maybe the few who know can tell us very well.

Let us all bring back fun to the Garrison again,

People just show up there, either sun or rain.

This is we Bajan thing and we can't let it die,

Remember our Grans who loved it too, even as the years did fly.

So lets support every time horse racing comes around,

Even at that special event when Gold Cup time abounds!

Barbados

Oh what a joy to live in this small, yet beautiful land,

A place where we can boast of with majestic crystal sand!

It's the place where I have been born, I've come to accept that,

Where coral and limestone uniquely meet firm black mould, though we flat.

Many of us never say no to the hard times we left behind,

When gran papa and mama work these lands, so lets respect their time.

Because of our past let's not forget the good works that lie ahead,

For it's our duty to fulfil this journey as we work for our daily bread.

One thing for sure about this great land, it brings out the best in us.

With such talent that stands among us, all only unity is a must.

Tribute to all who stand up tall who live by righteousness and truth,

With heads up high and forward on we are all but living proof.

We are the children that survive it all,

So with positiveness we can only stand tall.

After all respect to the land that you have been born,

And show only love from as early morn.

Lets try our best to do the best we can,

And however life comes respect God's plan.

Where Barbados Gone?

You who always seek to control mankind,

Long time now you love to be with the devil you dine.

We who now know before had never known the truth,

By the hands of your own you were sold from your youth.

So to control your money you have to tax the people hard,

Some of them as a youth you pitch marbles with in the yard.

Some real sad things with poor people happening around here,

With many still wondering why Barbados gone astray.

We in 2017 and our own making it harder than in slavery times,

Those who have it living sweet while others ain't got a dime.

All of those poor people pension cheques government playing truant with,

Those old people work extremely hard, to honour them should be our gift.

They are over taxing us so hard like they ain't care no more,

Still when election time come around will surely be knocking at your door.

In this twenty seventeen imagine poor people could hardly eat bread,

While big shots up in parliament playing politricks with people's head.

But dem ain't know that dem time coming real soon,

All they can say when that time comes that they give poor people gloom.

Who are these people fooling – could only be themselves,

Wearing their political masks running after their wealth.

Look how power and money can turn good people into fools,

Sitting in their hierarchical organizations treating poor people like mules.

Who living large off the poor surely can't do it all
the time,

One thing we know; we will always stand up for
truth and righteousness will be our sign!

Politics 2018

May 2018 and politics on we doorstep.

Poor people going through hardship still and ain't find no comforter yet.

All of the tax DLP[14] put on poor people backs and claim they ain't reach they gold,

Ask them where all of the money gone they could only tell you what they sold.

Who now is to take blame for our failing economy? Could never be poor people at all,

With all of the money they got stashed away, still no one to answer poor people's call.

Now all of the parties came on TV telling us of how much things they are going to do,

Never mentioning how they will free up poor people within their political brew.

The D's[15] say all of their finances are gone, now who is to be blame for that?

While poor people bellies falling in, yet all DLP members looking fat.

---

[14] DLP – Democratic Labour Party – one of the major political parties in Barbados
[15] D's – representing the DLP as above

The people like they want to give the B's[16] a chance
for the D's made poor people hear;

One old man said, "If ya let them back in we gine
graze grass," and he swear.

Looks like someone is playing the trump card
around here, for more lies are on the rise,

If the D's lose this election now to all Barbadians
that surely will be no surprise.

Boy, these DLP people have cause real uncertainty
right here in this land,

All poor people get was more promises and their
lives are like sinking sand.

So Ms. Mottley, if the people let you in, please give
them justice this time around,

Plus in history you will be our first lady PM and
you deserve to wear that crown.

---

[16] B's – representing the Barbados Labour Party, the other main political
party in Barbados

Tourist White Man

Tourist white man saw me on the beach one day,

Staring me down from head to toe and had something to say.

He said to his wife, "Check out that man, he like he is going mad!"

I now starting to get a little curious, for this starting to look real sad.

You know, I continue to do my thing, thinking some people ain't got a clue,

Of the real greatness of the Caribbean and the wonderful things we always do.

Some people will judge me by my looks and do not even know the man,

I was born and bred right here by this sea and on this sand.

Pure naturalness from youth every day I do intake,

True love and goodness I partake in only for righteousness sake.

Now he ain't know that acre that I do work in have in food of every kind,

And the sea I do dive in all types of fish I do find.

Then at the end I will then take a bath in one of
our sweet, wonderful springs,

So relaxing, so soothing, so much joy does it bring.

Mr Tourist Man you live in most concrete in your
material world,

Barbados is pure naturalness its a gem and a pear;

So you never judge a person by their looks my
friend,

And I will say it again and again: Barbados is a
pearl and a gem!

Chibim

Have you realise what CBC is doing these days?
We can now call this rock ChiBim;

Every time I turn on my TV all I could see is
Chinese film.

You could count them on your fingers the amount
of times these films show,

From morning even late in the night like they want
Bajans minds to blow.

We could as well buy a ticket and move there for
we are seeing them every day,

Stop children's show like once free Sesame Street
to see that now people have to pay.

This is a sad situation for the young and old; those
who can't afford have nothing to see,

Without cable, tell the youths to stay at home for
them that could never be.

So they are out there on the blocks, even in
vacation time, digesting only negative things.

Nothing more to do, only Chinese films to watch –
here is where the boring song sings.

Now how will you get them to stay at home
watching Chinese pictures every day?

They show on TV more than anything else, that's
the most that we can say.

That once Sunday evening matinee was always
sweet and special for us to see,

Now around that time the only thing they show is
'Wang shang we pang lee…'

Granny and Ms. Prime Minister

To our Prime Minister[17] I do give you congrats,

For trying to ease the load off of poor people backs.

Ma'am, you have now given poor people a little hope,

For the last ten years people's minds were up in smoke.

We pray and trust the gods for your sincerity,

To once again make poor people feel happy.

Now granny can eat a little better when she receives her pension again,

For before that granny had only pure pension pain.

Them old people work really hard to see better days come,

Ye they deserve to be treated better as their days begin to run.

There was a time when the old folks loved to watch 'Days Of Our Lives',

From six until seven in front of that TV most old folks would arrive.

---

[17] First female Prime Minister of Barbados, the Honourable Mia Amour Mottley

Just to hear them all chatting about the drama at show's end;

That show caused poor people who never spoke to become good friends.

Then all of a sudden they stop granny's favourite show,

Granny felt so bad she ask, "Why they had to treat old people so?"

That same show granny use to watch free for five nights,

You have to pay for now; for her, that could never be right.

So this is dedicated to Gran and my Prime Minister, you see,

Who have given Barbadians some hope for a better living – I, for sure, agree!

Our Prime Minister

Oh, look how our Prime Minister mek tears come from me eyes this day,

And it was all about de good things she had ta say.

How she would hear de poor people cry this time,

To bring back Barbados and again mek things real fine.

Man, she mek cold bumps come from ma head to ma toe,

To see someone finally care bout poor people so.

All Barbadians should thank her for at least making a try,

While others had our economy in a great dip and a sye[18].

Simple economics she brought for us all,

Not like others who had Barbados heading for a fall.

But thank God that we have few that still do care,

For poor people can be assured that they will be treated fair.

---

[18] Sye – sink, fall, descent (https://www.merriam-webster.com/dictionary/sye)

Madame Prime Minister, this budget that you talk
'bout make me stop and think,

We can see you are trying to pull back Barbados
that it would no longer sink.

So this is my request to each and every one,

Hold her up firmly, for this the land that we were
born.

We know there was another Prime Minister that
treated poor people this way,

Mr. Errol Barrow opened doors for poor people,
that I can surely say.

Sa far as real caring, very few played that role,

For all of de rest had poor people out in de cold.

So again, Madame Prime Minister, you are indeed a
true gem,

That's why all Barbadians should call you their
friend.

And we will surely support you all the way,

As Barbadians move forward each and every day.

Q in the Community

Q in the community, oh what a sweet place to be,

It doesn't matter if you are there in person or watching it on TV.

Now when you see these people stepping out,

Most of the time you have to hold ya mout'.

For that is where both grans go to have a good time,

We always know when they return – their faces always have a shine.

At Q you will find the old and young,

And if you love karaoke, pitch in and sing a song.

I do enjoy watching these people passionately enjoying themselves,

Instead of always staying home watching TV, like your life is on a lonely shelf.

It is good to get up get out go and interact with someone,

To stay at home and never go out, that surely can be a thorn.

Now everyone is dressed up and looking sweet, sweet, sweet,

And you know them old boys with their pants tucked in looking real neat.

Women with their hair styles around here looking extremely smart,

While food and drinks on sale even from de very start.

And the line dancing another sweet sight to watch,

One man shout to another, "I ain't drinking na rum, I drinking scotch!"

All now Q is pure enjoyment and a safe place to be,

Plus around here you can find almost every nationality;

With all my heart I know that Q is good for me and you,

So don't stop home, people, come out and join de Q crew.

We Gatherin' 2020

We Gatherin' Barbados[19] – to you, what does this mean?

Are your works still hidden or are there being seen?

To me it means to myself first I must be true,

My friends, don't wait or hesitate, to yourself you need to be, too.

Anything that will better people's lives especially that poor man out in the street,

Young and old, let's come together with love, embrace each other as we meet.

All of the violence and hatred that's in our land, it's time to bring it to an end,

Let go every malice against each other and let everyone be your friend.

'We Gatherin'' means let's gather as one; only love and unity will defeat all hate,

While we take that deep look within ourselves and let goodness be your fate.

---

[19] We Gatherin' 2020 – a Government initiative that was to symbolize a recommitment to the core values that make Barbados unique. It was to facilitate Barbadians from all over the world coming back home to Barbados for a year-long celebration, but was circumvented by the worldwide corona virus pandemic.

All of the events, please come out as we support one another,

With unity and strength we all must stand and show kindness to your sister and brother.

Let's spread our joy with the talent we have and show the world we will rebound,

With each one of us helping one another from our weaknesses we will be strong.

Remember people, as we gather together we are truly doing it for a good cause,

That our offspring to come will always go forward and will never be on pause.

And in turn we will be giving hope for many generations to come,

That equal rights and justice will stand for all and will forever be their sum.

GLOSSARY

Here are a list of words that are converted from common English into raw Bajan dialect, which is deliberately used in these poems. Many of the words in this book are spelled phonetically, and although they might be easily identifiable in context, they are still listed below for anyone who isn't a native Bajan speaker.

AH – I (as in 'ah can't forget dem days' – I can't forget…)

CAAN' – can't

GRANS – term of endearment for Granny/grandmother.

GINE – going

LAN'ING - landing

DE – the

TA/TUH – to

FA – for

NA – now, used for emphasis.

YEA – Yes

GAL   girl

GET PON – get on (in context, arrive)

WUK/WUKKING – work/working

MEK – Make, Makes

FA REAL – for truth, used for emphasis

DIS – this

DAT - that

DOLLA – dollar

DIN – didn't

NA – nah/didn't/haven't (as in na wuk: haven't worked); a term of negation

WA – what/well

DUN – finished

DEY – there

TIL – until

SA/SUH – so

SOME A WE – some of us

DUZ – do/does

BREK – having no money

WID – with

OVA – over

UM – it

PUN – on

WUNNA – you all

TEK - take

MASSA – master, used to identify the slave owners during the time of slavery